American Legends: The Life of Sidney Poitier

By Charles River Editors

Poitier in 2013

About Charles River Editors

Charles River Editors provides superior editing and original writing services across the digital publishing industry, with the expertise to create digital content for publishers across a vast range of subject matter. In addition to providing original digital content for third party publishers, we also republish civilization's greatest literary works, bringing them to new generations of readers via ebooks.

Sign up here to receive updates about free books as we publish them, and visit Our Kindle Author Page to browse today's free promotions and our most recently published Kindle titles.

Introduction

A picture of Poitier receiving the Presidential Medal of Freedom from President Obama

Sidney Poitier (1927-)

"In my case, the body of work stands for itself... I think my work has been representative of me as a man." – Sidney Poitier

"To be compared to Jackie Robinson is an enormous compliment, but I don't think it's necessarily deserved." – Sidney Poitier

A lot of ink has been spilled covering the lives of history's most influential figures, but how much of the forest is lost for the trees? In Charles River Editors' American Legends series, readers can get caught up to speed on the lives of America's most important men and women in the time it takes to finish a commute, while learning interesting facts long forgotten or never known.

Near the end of the 20th century, the American Film Institute ranked the greatest actors and actresses who worked during the Golden Era of Hollywood and the first half of the 1900s, and

Sidney Poitier was ranked 22nd among the men. Given the company he was surrounded by, such a distinction could be considered honor enough, but Poitier also happened to be the only minority on the list, an accomplishment made all the more incredible given the systematic discrimination he faced within the industry and the land where he grew up.

Though he spent much of his childhood in the Bahamas, Poitier was born in Miami and was exposed to the effects of Jim Crow at a young age, where he came face-to-face with Jim Crow. With no good educational opportunities, Poitier struggled to even learn how to read as a teen, and after a stint in the Army, it's unclear where his life was headed until he successfully auditioned for a spot in the American Negro Theater, an organization that staged plays during the 1940s and helped groom both Poitier and Harry Belafonte to be actors.

Poitier slowly but surely broke into Hollywood during the 1950s, becoming the first black man to be nominated for an Oscar for his role in *The Defiant Ones*. Naturally, many of Poitier's films dealt with the tensions of integration in America, and as he once noted, he was often "the only black person on the set. It was unusual for me to be in a circumstance in which every move I made was tantamount to representation of 18 million people." In 1964, at the height of the Civil Rights Movement, Poitier fittingly became the first black actor to win the Oscar for Best Actor thanks to his role in *Lilies of the Field*, and his best-known movie might be *Guess Who's Coming to Dinner*, which dealt with interracial relationships at a time when they were still controversial.

Today, Poitier is widely considered an American icon who helped break down barriers for minorities in Hollywood, and as a testament to courage and willpower in the face of discrimination off screen. He has been given too many honorary awards to count, and he recently received the Presidential Medal of Freedom in 2012. *American Legends: The Life of Sidney Poitier* chronicles the life and roles of the iconic actor. Along with pictures of important people, places, and events, you will learn about Poitier like never before, in no time at all.

American Legends: The Life of Sidney Poitier

About Charles River Editors

Introduction

Chapter 1: American Baby, Bahaman Boy

"The journey has been incredible from its beginning." – Sidney Poitier

From the very moment of his birth, Sidney Poitier was unique. Born in Miami on February 20, 1927, he grew up in the Bahamas, away from much of the uniquely American style of prejudice that pervaded the country at that time, especially the South. However, because of his premature birth in the United States, he also had the rights and privileges that went along with being an American citizen. He once explained, "My birth was quite unusual in that I was premature. I wasn't expected to live. I was delivered by a midwife in Miami, Florida…My parents were Bahamians…They farmed tomatoes and they sold their tomatoes in Miami, Florida…So it was that I was born in Florida unexpectedly. They had to keep me there for some three months, because I was so underprepared for birth that it took three months for me to hit a point at which they could take me on a sailboat, which would take several days back to the Bahamas and their tomato field."

Though he grew up away from American racism, Poitier also grew up away from the many material benefits that characterized the country of his accidental birth. In the 1930s, the Bahamas were still very primitive, even by the standards of the day, and most of the citizens, including Poitier's parents, were very poor. His father worked hard to provide for his wife and seven children, of whom Sidney was the youngest, and Poitier always admired his family. He said about his mother, "My mother was the most amazing person. She taught me to be kind to other women. She believed in family. She was with my father from the first day they met. All that I am, she taught me." Of his dad, Poitier added, "My father was a tomato farmer. There is the phrase that says he or she worked their fingers to the bone, well, that's my dad. And he was a very good man."

Nonetheless, it was a hard life marked by deprivation and sometimes even hunger. Poitier recalled, "We had roads, but they were pathways in a way. We had very little. I mean, we ate from the sea, food from the sea, and what they grew in their subsistence farming, in a particular way…There would be canned milk that would be shipped into the Bahamas from England. And there would be salt pork and salt beef and lard. We ate a lot of lard."

Poitier also received the first lessons of his limited education in their home town on Cat Island: "On Cat Island, there was a school house. The school house was a "multiple," meaning that there was one room. And the children, I don't think there were more than grade one to three, maybe four. And I went on Sundays. Other days I went to the farm…When there were available days for the school, I went to the school house." Eventually, Poitier's family moved to Nassau, the capital city, in 1937, and needless to say, it was a huge culture shock for the 10 year old boy. He would later recall, "There were windows along the streets on the main thoroughfare which was near the docks… And there were many things in the window…I was like a kid coming out of the center of the United States from the smallest, tiniest farming area and suddenly put into New

York City. That's the kind of impact, going into this whole new culture in Nassau."

Though new in town, Poitier had all the self-confidence that came from being the youngest and cherished child of a large family, and his likability led to his next big discovery in Nassau: "I met these new kids who were in this particular neighborhood, and they sort of embraced me. And they said to me… that they were going to a matinee, would I like to come? And I didn't want them to know that I didn't know what the word matinee meant. So I said, "Okay, sure." I want to be one of the group. So they went to this theater…the lights go down, and a curtain, big curtain thing opened up. And there was this big white frame. And suddenly, out of nowhere, came letters, big letters, words, on this big, white screen…I couldn't make out really what the words were saying, except some of them were names…But then I saw people, and it shocked me. How did they get there? Then I saw cows and I saw wagons and I saw brown people wearing skins and feathers…That was my first movie."

Needless to say, Poitier was mesmerized, but he was also confused. In fact, he was so shook up by what he had just seen that he returned to the theater later just to try to figure out what he had actually seen. He explained, "I went to the back of the theater, because I didn't understand how all those cows and the people and -- how did they get the houses in that little building where I was?...In the back of the theater was a door, just a door. It was too tiny for all those cows to come through. I didn't understand, but I thought that something was going to come out of there."

Of course, there was much more to Poitier's young life than going to movies, because he soon had to drop out of school to work and help support his family. He remembered, "I went to a school there in Nassau, but I wasn't very successful at that. Then the fragility of my parents' economic situation forced me to go to work…First I went to work as a water boy, working on a construction thing…But it didn't pay very much, and my folks really were in need, so I decided that I was tall enough to hike my age and maybe get a job as an adult. I went to the assistant to the foreman…I was among the big guys, and I was using a pick axe and shoveling dirt up out of this ditch, up onto the region up above it. And because the pay was much, much better…it was very helpful for food and all that stuff…I stayed at that job, and then I worked as a delivery boy, and then I worked in a warehouse."

Chapter 2: The Land of Opportunity

"I couldn't adjust to the racism in Florida. It was so blatant...I had never been so described as Florida described me."

"I lived in a country where I couldn't live where I wanted to live. I lived in a country where I couldn't go where I wanted to eat. I lived in a country where I couldn't get a job, except for those put aside for people of my colour or caste."

Decades later, Poitier would look back and reflect on how the Bahamas shaped his childhood and outlook on life, calling the life there "simple" but also explaining how people took care of each other: "But that strong sense of self-worth came from the Bahamas itself, out of my family, out of the families I knew. Out of the society, such as it was. But they treated each other respectfully, they raised their children to be respectful of elders. If my mother was unable to work in the fields, her friends would come by and bring food. It was a wonderful community. When we got to Nassau, it was somewhat different, but still...So as a kid I didn't run around being fearful that I was going to be mistreated. Okay, that gives you an idea of what I came out of, and the values I came out of the Bahamas with…"

However, by the time Poitier was 15, it was obvious to his family that there was no future for him in Nassau. His young friends were beginning to get in trouble with the law, and his father was concerned that he might join them. Furthermore, the senior Poitier was also concerned that Sidney was not getting enough to eat; his work as a cab driver provided a lifestyle that allowed the family to barely subsist, and he understandably wanted more for his youngest son. Meanwhile, his oldest son, Cyril, was writing encouraging letters from his new home in the United States, and since Sidney was already an American citizen, it made all kinds of sense to send him to live with his brother. Thus, Poitier left the Bahamas in 1942 for a new life in America: "My oldest brother had stowed away on a motorboat that ran between Nassau and Florida…He found a job and he worked very hard. Tremendous guy, this guy was. Cyril was his name. He met a girl, fell in love with her and she with him and they got married and he went down to the police station in the center of Miami and he told them that he was a stowaway and that he has been here such and such a time and he explained to them what he did…I don't know what the circumstances were, but they allowed him to stay, and I was sent to him."

Poitier could not have arrived in the United States at a better time economically, as World War II had drawn away many young men into the army and created job opportunities for those left at home. Furthermore, he believed he "had learned something of Miami from people who had visited there, so I knew what to expect." However, while Sidney quickly found a job as a delivery boy for Burdines department store, he learned some hard lessons about American race relations almost immediately: "A lady came to the door, a white lady. And she said, 'Yes?' And I said, 'Ma'am this is your package. I come from Burdines department store.' She looked at me in the most amazing way and she said, 'Get around to the back.' And I didn't understand, I really didn't understand it, because she's standing right there…She slammed the door in my face. And I took the package and I set it right down on the step in front of the house and I left…Now, I'm going home to my brother's house…And then the door suddenly opens and it's my sister-in-law…grabs me and pulls me into the house, slams the door, and on the floor she's lying with her children. And she pulls me down and she said, 'What did you do today?' I said, 'What did I do? What do you mean?' She explained to me that the Klan had come to the house looking for me, because I had misbehaved I guess."

Needless to say, this experience soured Poitier on Miami, even though he had encountered racism back in Nassau. He explained, "I didn't run into racism until we moved to Nassau when I was ten and a half, but it was vastly different from the kind of horrendous oppression that black people in Miami were under when I moved there at 15. I found Florida an antihuman place." As a result, he began to make plans on how to get out, and he was buoyed by hearing stories about New York City, particularly a neighborhood there called Harlem. Poitier heard about the opportunities there for people of color, so he made up his mind to get there. For two years, he worked hard and saved his money until he was finally able to get out, but the trip was more of an odyssey than he could ever have imagined. He recalled, "I took a bus from Florida, and I went to Atlanta. They transferred me to another bus that went to another place, close to the foot of the mountains, and someone met me there and took me up the mountain…I spent much of that summer there, all within the same year…And when I left there, I had $39."

That ordeal proved to be just the beginning for Poitier, who had to adjust to the city environment itself: "New York was an experience. It was a staggering experience. It was massive. It was huge. There were incredibly tall buildings. I got there in the afternoon, and the place I wanted to go to was Harlem, to see Harlem. I had heard a great deal about Harlem…So I got on the train. And every time it stopped, I was amazed. How could it be running under the ground? Makes no sense to me. But I'm alert, and I'm sitting there. And I see the station comes up, 116th Street. And I jumped off, and I walked and followed people going up the steps. And I walked out at 116th Street and 8th Avenue, and I was in Harlem."

Poitier quickly began to assimilate into his new community, later recalling, "I did learn early that everything I want to do in life requires that I accumulate understanding, knowledge, know-how. What is the quickest, most dimensional way to make that kind of accumulation? You have to read…The first place I went to was to newspapers." Unfortunately, at that point, Poitier had yet to really learn how to read, but thankfully, a kind stranger would soon set him on the path to literacy and success: "I was a dishwasher…And I'm reading one of the papers. And there was a Jewish waiter sitting at the table, elderly man, and he saw me there. He got up, and he walked over…and he said, 'Hi.' And I looked up, and I said, 'Hi.' He said, 'What's new in the papers?' And I said to him, 'I can't tell you what's new in the papers because I don't read very well…' He said, 'Ah,' he said, 'Well, would you like me to read with you?' And I accepted…Every night after that, he would come over and sit with me, and he would teach me about what a comma is and why it exists, what periods are, what colons are, what dashes are. He would teach me that there are syllables, and how to differentiate them in a single word, and consequently learn how to pronounce them. Every night."

Even while he was washing dishes, Poitier could not help but think he was meant for something better. In the back of his mind, there was always the story his mother had told him about the dark days right after his premature birth, when it looked like he might not survive: "[S]he decided to stop in and visit a soothsayer…And… she looked at my mother and she said, 'Don't worry about your son. He will survive, and he will not be a sickly child. You must not worry about that child.'…She told my mother that I would travel to all the corners of the earth, I will walk with kings, I will be rich and famous."

Chapter 3: Actor Wanted

"I decided in my life that I would do nothing that did not reflect positively on my father's life." – Sidney Poitier

"The acting came totally as an accident…There's an African American paper called the Amsterdam News…And something caught my eye. And what caught my eye was a phrase. It said, 'Actors Wanted.'…But what is this actor's job? That doesn't sound like it's too bad. And, they're inviting me because they say actors wanted. There was an address there in the article. It was just ten blocks away. I knocked on the door, and a guy came to the door, opened it. It was the basement of a library, and this was the headquarters of the American Negro Theatre." - Sidney Poitier

Poitier got his first big break when he was accepted into the American Negro Theatre in 1944, even though he "was not looking to be an actor. I was not looking for opportunities. I had absolutely no interest at all in being an actor. I was a dishwasher. I was, at that point, content to be a dishwasher because I felt and understood and embraced the fact that I did not have the wherewithal to do much else. I wanted to do more. Not only did I want to do more, I was preparing myself to do more." Naturally, one of the ways in which Poitier prepared himself for a life as an actor was continuing to practice his reading: "I had great problems with pronouncing three syllables. And every word that had three, four syllables in it, it staggered me. I mean it just defeated me. So I decided that I had to learn to read better because all of the information necessary for my survival came to me, would come to me in words. I knew if I didn't understand the words, I wouldn't know the message. And if I don't know the message, no one will have time for me."

Once inside the door at the American Negro Theater, Poitier was soon grateful that he had been practicing his reading, since the man who answered the door immediately thrust a script in his hand. Still, his nerves and his natural insecurity about his education initially caused problems: "I am very slow. And I am very particular in trying to pronounce these three syllable words and four syllable words. As a result I'm saying, 'When-are-you-going-to-be...' He said, 'You can't read, you can hardly talk,' cause I had this accent, you know…He opened the door, pushed me out. Slammed the door…I did decide then, at that moment, on that street, that I am going to be an actor just to show him that he was wrong about me. And then I would give up the acting, because what do I want to be an actor for?"

From the beginning of his career, Poitier was determined to never take a part that he felt in any way diminished his sense of who he was, because, as he once put it, "[W]ho I am is my father's son. That's who I am. And I spent my life with him until I left him at the age of 15. And I've seen him behave with my mother and their children. And I've seen him with my mother, how he treats her. I grew up on that. I know how to be a decent human being." However, before he could worry about the roles he played, he had to get one. Determined, Poitier returned to the American Negro Theatre, but this time prepared to audition. Not knowing where to purchase a script with a scene he could master, he instead learned two paragraphs out of the popular woman's magazine *True Confessions.* Perhaps not surprisingly, he was not accepted into the program after his first unconventional reading, so he went back to the school and made a unique proposal: "I said, 'I noticed that you don't have a janitor.' And I said, 'I will do the janitor work for you because it's not a big deal, you know, you have a fairly small place here and stuff. I will do the janitor work for you in exchange for letting me study here.' And she looked at me in a peculiar way. She said, 'You would do that?' I said, 'Yes, I would do that.'…I went back in three days,…and she comes out with a guy…He said, 'You would do that?' I said, 'Yes, I would do that.' He said, 'Why would you do that?' I said, 'Because I want to learn. I want to learn.'…Well, they let me in."

Poitier's troubles did not end when he got into the school, because even though he was literally willing to work from the ground up, he was asked to leave not long after he started because the teachers felt he showed no promise. However, he was popular among the other students, some of whom went to bat for him and convinced the administration to let him return even though they still didn't think he had the makings of an actor. Poitier explained, "So, she said to me, 'I'll let you understudy the guy who's gonna play the part.' Now, she had no intentions of me ever, ever playing that part…The guy that she had chosen to do the part was Harry Belafonte, a very handsome, well-known, good actor. Anyway, long story short, I studied that part, and I was on top of it as best I could. The evening of the performance, Harry Belafonte unfortunately could not come…I went on, I played the part, I knew all the words. I had my accent, you know, and I did the best I could."

Belafonte

As fate would have it, there was a Broadway producer in the audience that night who liked Poitier's performance, so afterwards, the producer approached Poitier and invited him to audition for *Lysistrata*, an ancient Greek play he was casting at that time. Poitier got the role, but he soon learned that there was a lot more to acting than he had originally thought: "I was so frightened, I was so petrified, that I started it, but instead of starting with my first line, I started with my seventh or eighth line. And the guy who was supposed to answer me, his eyes went BOING! And he said, 'Uhh...' And he takes his line, goes back and pulls up the response to this line, and it got all (mixed up)...Well, the critics said, several of them said, 'Who was this kid who walked out there and opened this play? He was full of humor...'"

Though *Lysistrata* closed after only three days, it led to Poitier landing a job as an understudy in *Anna Lucasta*, which would prove to be his big break and a production that he would work on here and there throughout much of his stage career. He had to return to washing dishes after the first run of *Anna Lucasta* ended, but his integrity regarding which roles he took worked in Poitier's favor by bringing him to the attention of the popular acting agent Martin Baum, who told him, "I have never been able to understand why you turned down that job for $700. I have decided that anyone as crazy as you are, I want to be their agent." In fact, Baum would remain Poitier's agent for the rest of his career and was one of the people most responsible for his success.

Another person who contributed to Poitier's early success was his wife, Juanita, whom he married in 1950. They went on to have four daughters together during their early years together, but with Poitier struggling to get his acting career off the ground, he and his wife steadily grew apart over time.

Chapter 4: Learning the Meaning

"I learned so much. I learned from them that behind words are meanings. Every word has a meaning, and its meaning might simply be used as a connection: is, as, was, then, now, last, first. There's a meaning. Now, when we put words together, if we don't express what the meaning is behind this particular bunch of words as actors, if we cannot articulate what is behind this bunch of words -- which would be maybe just one paragraph -- behind it may be one point of view or it may be a combination of points of views. The audience hearing these would expect to see them exemplified in the behavior of the actor." - Sidney Poitier

"If the screen does not make room for me in the structure of their screenplay, I'll step out. I'll step back. I'd step back. I couldn't do it. I just couldn't do it." – Sidney Poitier

With Baum's help, Poitier landed his first significant role in *No Way Out* (1950), in which he played a doctor trying to serve the neediest people in a large city slum. A critic for *The New York Times* praised his performance, writing, "Sidney Poitier gives a fine, sensitive performance as the Negro doctor and his quiet dignity is in sharp, affecting contrast to the volatile, sneering, base animal mentality and vigor that Mr. (Richard) Widmark expresses so expertly as Ray Biddle." From there, Poitier went on to star in the classic *Cry, the Beloved Country* (1951) and *The Red Ball Express* (1952). He even appeared with the newly launched Harlem Globetrotters in *Go, Man, Go!* (1954).

However, it was his role as a struggling student in *Blackboard Jungle* (1955) that proved to be his big break. As one critic wrote, "Vic Morrow, as the most rebellious pupil, is a sinister replica of a Marlon Brando roughneck, and Sidney Poitier, as the approachable Negro, is exceedingly sharp and alert. As individuals, these two performers would seem superlatively realistic types…"

From there, Poitier went on to receive his first nomination for a BAFTA Award for Best Actor in a Leading Role for his performance in *Edge of the City* (1957), but since the studio was concerned that they would not be able to market the film in the South, MGM only budgeted $500,000 to make the movie. For this, his first starring role, Poitier was paid a mere $15,000. The movie was ahead of its time in portraying an interracial relationship in which both parties were at least somewhat equal. It was also noteworthy that the movie hinted at John Cassavetes' character being gay, to the extent that The Motion Picture Production Code Administration demanded "extremely careful handling to avoid planting the suspicion that he may be homosexual." Regardless, *Time* praised Poitier's performance, saying his character "is not only the white man's boss, but is his best friend, and is at all times his superior, possessing greater intelligence, courage, understanding, warmth and general adaptability."

Ruby Dee, Poitier and John Cassavetes in the trailer for *Edge of the City*

Poitier's next significant movie, *The Mark of the Hawk*, saw him receive second billing in the closing credits, and even though the more prominent opening credits listed him fourth, it was nonetheless an achievement for a person of color in late 1950s America.

Though viewers would never know it by watching them, Poitier's next two films, *The Defiant Ones* (1958) and *Porgy and Bess* (1959), were secretly linked because Poitier only agreed to be in *Porgy* so that he could star in *The Defiant Ones*. He later explained, "I was in the Caribbean making a picture with John Cassavetes. There was no telephone on the island, so I would take a four-hour trip to St. Thomas and go to a hotel to call home, then my agent. On one such trip, Marty said, 'We've got a problem.' His West Coast co-agent had gotten a call from [film producer] Sam Goldwyn, who had said, 'I want Sidney Poitier to play Porgy. Can you get him for me?' and the co-agent said, 'I'll get him for you.' That went public quickly, and mind you, I'm away, so I don't know anything about this. After Marty told me, I said, 'Just call Mr. Goldwyn and tell him that I'm not going to play the part. And Goldwyn said to Marty, 'Why don't you have Sidney come out and talk with me, and if he tells me that he doesn't want to do it, then I'll know that he means it.'"

SAMUEL GOLDFISH
General Manager and Treasurer
Jesse Lasky Feature Film Co.

Samuel Goldwyn

This seemed like a reasonable idea, and that is what Poitier planned to do by just showing up and explain to Goldwyn that he was tone deaf and therefore unsuitable to be cast as the lead in a musical. He recalled, "So when I finished my movie, I went to California to see Sam. And I told him as respectfully as I could that I couldn't play the part. He said, 'Do me a favor: Go back to New York and think about it for two weeks.' And I said, 'But I know now!' And he said, 'Just think about it.'"

That is when the stakes of the game changed: "When I went back to my hotel, there was a script waiting for me called *The Defiant Ones*. I read the script in one sitting and said to Marty, 'This is something I'd like to do. Tell Mr. Goldwyn that I'd like to meet with Stanley Kramer'—the guy who wants me to do this movie. So I went to see Stanley, and he said, 'I would love to have you play in it, but you have a problem—Sam Goldwyn.' Sam was one of the most powerful men in the entire industry. And having gone public with the news that I may play the Porgy role, he had put himself on the line. So I got a call from Hedda Hopper [the famous Hollywood columnist]. She said, 'I know Sam, and he's in a tough position. If you don't do his picture, he'll see to it that you never work in this town again.' So I had a lot of thinking to do, and I agonized. And I couldn't come to a conclusion." It didn't help that at the time, as Poitier later conceded, "I was not the kind of a principal player that was so in demand that eight or 10 or 12 scripts came per month."

Hedda Hopper

As would happen again and again in his career, Baum stepped in to help Poitier make the right decision: "Finally, Marty and I came up with the only thing I could do, because I wanted to do *The Defiant Ones*. I did one movie, *Porgy and Bess*, so I could do the other. It was painful, but it was useful. I learned some lessons, and if I had it to do again, I wouldn't do it any differently, because I had work to do."

Not only did he have the work itself, but Poitier also enjoyed making *The Defiant Ones*, later explaining, "It was a wonderful experience for me because it was produced and directed by a great filmmaker named Stanley Kramer...He was one of Hollywood's most liberal, most courageous men in the business, particularly during a delicate time in America. Working for him was pleasure, a total pleasure." Poitier's work showed well on screen and his role won him his first BAFTA Award and a Silver Bear, both for Best Actor. He also became the first male actor of African descent to be nominated for an Oscar for Best Actor, and he was nominated for a Golden Globe as well. The often critical Bosley Crowther of *The New York Times* praised Poitier for showing "a deep and powerful strain of underlying compassion," and *Variety* wrote, "Poitier captures all of the moody violence of the convict, serving time because he assaulted a white man who had insulted him. It is a cunning, totally intelligent portrayal that rings powerfully true."

Kramer

Poitier and Tony Curtis in *The Defiant Ones*

From this point forward, Poitier would be at the forefront of American cinema for the next decade.

Chapter 5: Playing to the Five Senses

"Every person who goes into a theater -- and anyone who … is interested in theater or the creative arts -- anyone interested in theater arts, they enter a movie house, or they enter a theater with a stage, they sit there with other people, it's a darkened room. Their attention is on what's going on up there. They have five senses that are the tools they bring into the theater. They know, feel, touch. They know what they see objectively. They know what they hear. So their five senses are working, and they've been working pretty much since they were tots. So everything that happens on that stage, everything that happens on that screen, they can pass a judgment subconsciously as to whether we are hitting the marks or not." - Sidney Poitier

"The impact of the black audience is expressing itself. They look to films to be more expressive of their needs, their lives. Hollywood has gotten that message - finally." – Sidney Poitier

Poitier returned to Broadway in 1959 to star as Walter Lee Younger in *A Raisin in the Sun*, a show that ran for more than 15 months and earned him a Tony nomination for Best Actor. He later starred in the movie version and earned nominations for both a BAFTA and a Golden Globe for Best Actor. He later remembered, "Lloyd Richards was the director of *A Raisin in the Sun*. And he was more than a director. He was a theater master, master of theater. African American, extremely gifted. He and a man named Paul Mann, they were teachers. They had a teaching -- a drama school, actually...I went to see them because I knew I wasn't working at the level I should be working at...I asked them if I could come and take some classes, and they said yes. They invited me in. I stayed there for a very long time. And they taught me."

Picture of Poitier in the stage version of *A Raisin in the Sun*

In between, Poitier starred as a young soldier fighting in the Korean War in *All the Young Men*, a role author Hall Barlett wrote especially for him. However, Columbia Pictures insisted that Poitier have a white co-star, and no actor would step forward to take the part. Finally, Alan Ladd, who was co-producing the film, agreed to play opposite him. Years later, Poitier was forgiving of his fellow actors and the time in which they lived, telling Oprah Winfrey, "It was difficult. We were so new in Hollywood. There was almost no frame of reference for us except as stereotypical, one-dimensional characters. Not only was I not going to do that, but I had in mind what was expected of me—not just what other blacks expected but what my mother and father expected. And what I expected of myself."

Alan Ladd

After starring in *Pressure Point* (1962), a psychodrama in which Poitier portrayed a psychiatrist working with a prison inmate, he went on to make *The Long Ships* (1963), the only other role he ever took against his will. Poitier's distaste for his role as a seafaring Moor shows in his performance, and the movie was not very well-received, but better things were just around the corner.

Poitier's performance as a young African-American man helping a group of European nuns build a church in *Lilies of the Field* (1963) marked not only the pinnacle of his own career but a turning point in Hollywood. The performance earned him his first Academy Award, and it was the first Oscar for Best Actor ever given to an actor of color at that. Indeed, no African-American had won an Oscar in the nearly 25 years since Hattie McDaniel won an Oscar as a supporting actress for her portrayal of Mammy in *Gone With the Wind* (1939), and Poitier's character was certainly nobody's mammy, as he was quick to point out: "It was pretty much how I am. And what it meant to me to receive the award for it, it meant a great deal to me. It was the first time for an African American. I thoroughly, thoroughly enjoyed the experience, because what he was doing -- the character mind you -- what he was doing was exhibiting a vast sense of himself, and the wonders of being alive, and the wonders of being a human being, and the responsibilities of a human being. And here he is vortexing with some of the most loveable characters. And for that I got an award. I embraced the award. It was wonderful."

Poitier later expressed his appreciation to the "man who wanted so badly to make that movie, did in fact, direct it. Ralph Nelson. I've made movies for him in my career several times, three times, as a matter of fact. Ralph Nelson was a very, very, very humane person. He hired me for three fantastic roles. I will always be indebted to Ralph Nelson because he was a real humanitarian." Still, his biggest delight was to know how much his win meant to his mother: "She lived long enough to see me win the Academy Award. And that was tremendous…When I arrived in Nassau, the people gave me a parade around the island, and she thought that was swell. The thing that best describes my mother is that, subsequent to me winning the Academy Award, she would go around the neighborhood, and whenever she'd see a mother chastising her kid, she would say, 'You be careful with that child—my Sidney used to act that way.'"

In addition to winning the Oscar, Poitier also won both a Golden Globe Award and a Silver Bear for Best Actor, as well as receiving nominations for a BAFTA Award for Best Actor in a Leading Role, a Laurel Award for Top Male Dramatic Performance, and a New York Film Critics Circle Award for Best Actor. Decades later, the American Film Institute named his character, Homer Smith, one of its top 50 movie heroes.

Chapter 6: Overcoming On Screen and Off

"There isn't a person that sits in a movie house, of any maturity, who hasn't been disappointed, who hasn't been exhilarated, who hasn't felt fear, who hasn't felt joy. Every one of the emotions that human beings experience, even the most terrifying ones, they have been akin to all of them at one time or another, either in their daily lives, their weekly lives, their monthly lives, their yearly lives. So that when they sit in that theater, that's all they bring in. That's the scoreboard they bring in. And they sit there and they watch actors playing at fear, embarrassment, at love, at hate, at all of the emotions in life…And that's the actor's job…And one by one, this really fine actress or actor begins to do things that somewhere in the consciousness of that audience, they're saying, 'Ooh boy, yeah, I know about that. I've seen that. Wow.'" - Sidney Poitier

In spite of his delight over winning the Oscar, Poitier expressed concern that he might now find it more difficult to receive offers for good roles. In particular, he was afraid that since Hollywood could now rest on the fact a black man had won an Oscar, the industry need not do anything else to promote racial equality. At first, it seemed that Poitier's fears were destined to be realized, because he was subsequently cast in softball roles in *The Bedford Incident* (1965) and *The Slender Thread* (1965), as well as playing Simon the Cyrene in *The Greatest Story Ever Told* (1965). The stress took a toll on his marriage; he and his wife, Juanita, divorced in 1965, and he struggled to remain active in the lives of his four daughters: Beverly, Pamela, Sherri and Gina.

Poitier once noted that if people "apply reason and logic to this career of mine, you're not going to get very far," and that seemed to be the case until he re-entered the world of racial tension in *A Patch of Blue* (1965), which had him play an African-American man who falls in love with a young white woman who is blind. The film itself was designed to show the state of race relations in the United States and was deliberately filmed in black-and-white to draw attention to the film's theme. The scene in which the two kiss was cut from the versions of the movie that were released in the South, but otherwise, everyone's work paid off because it became the most financially successful film of Poitier's career and earned him nominations for a BAFTA, a Golden Globe and a Laurel Award. It also cemented him as one of Hollywood's biggest box office draws.

The mid-1960s were incredibly turbulent times in America, and the long-festering issue of race was finally tackled head on during the Civil Rights Movement. As is always the case during times of change, many innocent people, even those trying desperately to do the right thing, got caught in the crossfire of accusations and attempts at solutions. Sidney Poitier was one of those who seemed to be unable to please anybody; white racists thought he was not being kept in his place, while some ardent civil rights activists thought he was too complacent with his place in life. Decades later, he reflected, "Even Dr. King was branded an Uncle Tom because of the rage…I lived through people turning on me. It was painful for a couple years…I was the most successful black actor in the history of the country. I was not in control of the kinds of films I would be offered, but I was totally in control of the kinds of films I would do. So I came to the mix with that power—the power to say, 'No, I will not do that.' I did that from the beginning. Back then, Hollywood was a place in which there had never been a *To Sir, With Love*, *The Defiant Ones*, *In the Heat of the Night* or *Guess Who's Coming to Dinner*. Nothing like it. What the name-callers missed was that the films I did were designed not just for blacks but for the mainstream. I was in concert with maybe a half-dozen filmmakers, and they were all white. And they chose to make films that would make a statement to a mainstream audience about the awful nature of racism."

Poitier with Belafonte and Charlton Heston during the Civil Rights March on Washington, D.C. in 1963

In fact, many others were raising concerns about the roles Poitier was choosing to play, and Poitier was concerned as well, albeit for a different reason. While he liked the idea of playing complicated, even evil characters, he also felt an obligation to be the kind of example for other minorities that his parents were for him. For decades, members of racial minorities had been portrayed in such a negative way that he wanted to use his influence to portray his characters as solid citizens.

As it turned out, *A Patch of Blue* was only the first in a series of highly successful films that Poitier starred in. After making *Duel at Diablo* (1966), he went on to star in *To Sir, with Love*

(1967), which cast him as a struggling high school teacher dealing with a white female student who had a crush on him. *To Sir, with Love* proved to be financial hit that netted nearly $42 million, and it also made Poitier a millionaire because his contract gave him 10% of the movie's gross revenue.

According to Crowther, the movie had "a nice air of gentility suffuses this pretty color film, and Mr. Poitier gives a quaint example of being proper and turning the other cheek. Although he controls himself with difficulty in some of his confrontations with his class, and even flares up on one occasion, he never acts like a boor, the way one of his fellow teachers (played by Geoffrey Bayldon) does. Except for a few barbed comments by the latter, there is little intrusion of or discussion about the issue of race: It is as discreetly played down as are many other probable tensions in this school. To Sir, with Love comes off as a cozy, good-humored and unbelievable little tale." However, other critics were not so kind; *The Monthly Film Bulletin* said "the sententious script sounds as if it has been written by a zealous Sunday school teacher after a particularly exhilarating boycott of South African oranges."

Poitier's next film, *In the Heat of the Night* (1967) was also highly successful among critics and at the box office, but it proved to be a very stressful film for the actor to make because it dredged up a number of personal issues that he might have preferred to keep buried. The most difficult issue came up while he was preparing to do a scene in which his character was slapped by a white man: "The scene required me to stand there, this guy walks over to me, and he slaps me in the face. And I look at him fiercely and walk away. And I said to Walter, I said, 'You can't do that.'...I said, 'The black community will look at that and say that is egregious. You can't do that, because the human responses that would be natural in that circumstance, we are suppressing them to serve values of greed on the part of Hollywood, acquiescence on the part of people culturally who would accept that as the proper approach.' I said, 'You can't do it.' I said, 'You certainly won't do it with me.' I talked to him about it. I say, 'Therefore, if you want me to do this, not only will I not do it, but I will insist that I respond to this man precisely as a human being would ordinarily respond to this man. And he pops me, and I'll pop him right back.'"

Poitier won the day, and the powerful scene was filmed as he requested. The movie and his role as Virgil Tibbs went on to inspire two sequels: *They Call Me MISTER Tibbs!* (1970) and *The Organization* (1971). It also inspired a popular television series starring Carroll O'Connor and Howard Rollins as Tibbs.

Chapter 7: Connectedness

"But what I learned was not in terms of something I got out of a book. What I learned was an internal connectedness to life, in the family, in the small community where we lived, how people treated each other, particularly how my father treated his friends and my mother, you see. So I came at 15 to Miami, Florida with a sense of that humanity. That is why I am sitting in this chair now. All of what I feel about life, I had to find a way in my work to be faithful to it, to be respectful of it. I couldn't and still can't play a scene, I cannot play a scene that I don't find the texture of humanity in the material. I can't." - Sidney Poitier

Guess Who's Coming to Dinner (1967), directed by Stanley Kramer, proved to be one of the most powerful and memorable movies of Poitier's career. Designed to face the racist tendencies present in even the most liberal Americans, it starred Poitier as the perfect young suitor of an upper-middle class white girl. He was a good-looking doctor, well-educated, and wholesome, even refusing to give into his fiancée's desire for premarital sex. Subsequent critics have complained that Poitier's character was literally too good to be true, and that his background and resume were too perfect for any actual human being.

Of course, the rub in the movie was that this ideal young suitor was black, which sets the stage for one confrontation after another throughout the film when the girl brings him to meet her family. Poitier even noted that when Katharine Hepburn and Spencer Tracy were slated to play the girl's parents, Poitier felt like he was "under close observation" by the two, but that they came to like him and gave him "the kind of respect they had for Kramer, and they had to say to themselves (and I'm sure they did), this kid has to be pretty okay, because Stanley is nuts about working with him."

The only thing that rivaled the importance of Poitier's performance is that it was the last time Hollywood legends Spencer Tracy and Katharine Hepburn worked together, as Tracy died shortly after filming. In fact, Tracy's poor health nearly jeopardized the project before it even got off the ground, as Kramer explained, "You're never examined for insurance until a few weeks before a picture starts. With all his drinking and ailments, Tracy always qualified for insurance before, so nobody thought it would be a problem in this case. But it was. We couldn't get insurance for Spence. The situation looked desperate. So then we figured out a way of handling it. Kate and I put up our own salaries to compensate for the lack of an insurance company for Spence. And we were allowed to proceed."

Poitier later talked about working with the dying Tracy: "The illness of Spencer dominated everything. I knew his health was very poor and many of the people who knew what the situation was didn't believe we'd finish the film, that is, that Tracy would be able to finish the film. Those of us who were close knew it was worse than they thought. Kate brought him to and from the set. She worked with him on his lines. She made sure with Kramer that his hours were right for what he could do, and what he couldn't do was different each day. There were days when he couldn't do anything. There were days when he was great, and I got the chance to know what it was like working with Tracy."

Katharine Hepburn and Spencer Tracy in *Guess Who's Coming to Dinner*

In fact, Poitier was in such awe of his co-stars that he once found it difficult to remember his lines during a scene with the two: "When I went to play a scene with Tracy and Hepburn, I couldn't remember a word. Finally Stanley Kramer said to me, 'What are we going to do?' I said, 'Stanley, send those two people home. I will play the scene against two empty chairs. I don't want them here because I can't handle that kind of company.' He sent them home. I played the scene in close-up against two empty chairs as the dialogue coach read Mr. Tracy's and Miss Hepburn's lines from off camera."

While the film itself won quite a few awards, including an Oscar for Best Picture, Poitier was largely ignored by awards committees, but his success in *Guess Who's Coming to Dinner* earned him many new privileges as an actor. One of these was the chance to write his own material, and with the help of experienced screenwriter Robert Alan Arthur, he wrote the script for the movie *For Love of Ivy* (1968), in which he also starred. The movie was very popular with viewers of all races, perhaps because of the comedic relationship the black characters shared with their white counterparts. Though not a huge hit, it did make a decent profit, especially for such a small film.

In spite of his success on the big screen, Poitier continued to be targeted by those who felt that he was still not doing enough, and his next movie, *The Lost Man* (1969), was surprisingly unpopular with the critics, one of whom complained, "Sidney Poitier does not make movies, he makes milestones. It is not necessarily his fault, but rather it is the result of an accident of timing combined with his affinity for working with second-rate directors. Because he is black, as well as a major movie star, his movies require social interpretations that have nothing to do with cinema, which is ironic since Poitier has never made a movie that revealed anything as important about America as his success in it. He is a good actor but it is his career that's important. The best of his movies—most recently, 'For Love of Ivy' and 'In the Heat of the Night'—are of interest only as pleasant, conventional entertainments."

Unfortunately, the bad reviews kept coming, even with the sequel to his very popular *In the Heat of the Night*. *They Call Me MISTER Tibbs!* (1970) was supposed to triumphantly resurrect the popular police detective to cheers of adoration, but instead, one reviewer snarled, "Whether good or bad, almost every movie Sidney Poitier has made has been a kind of elegant sit-in, an act of conscience that quite measurably increased the opportunities available to all other black actors. With 'They Call Me Mister Tibbs!' Poitier establishes another inalienable right, that of the black movie star to make the sort of ordinary, ramshackly entertaining, very close to pointless movie that a white movie star like Frank Sinatra has been allowed to get away with for most of his career. Actually, this may be one of the most important rights of all, for eventually it should allow Poitier to behave less like a solemn abstraction for achievement and more like a real, vulnerable man."

Chapter 8: Directing

"So I had to be careful. I recognized the responsibility that, whether I liked it or not, I had to accept whatever the obligation was. That was to behave in a manner, to carry myself in such a professional way, as if there ever is a reflection, it's a positive one." – Sidney Poitier

After Poitier's next two movies, *Brother John* (1971) and *The Organization* (1971), were released, it was obvious that he was going to have to make some major changes if he was going to continue to have a successful career in Hollywood. Thus, he followed in the path of many actors who came before and after him and decided to try his hand at directing. He explained, "I decided that I must learn everything I could about the production of motion pictures. In a way, I had always been doing that by watching directors, but I decided I wanted to make films. I entered an agreement with Paul Newman, Steve McQueen and Barbra Streisand. We started a film production company called First Artists. I did four movies with them. I did Uptown Saturday Night, Let's Do It Again and A Piece of the Action. I did A Warm December as well. I set out to make films that would get people to laugh at themselves without cringing. Then I went on to direct other films, such as Stir Crazy."

By the mid-1970s, Poitier had become something of an elder statesman among African-American actors, and in that capacity, he was able to attract some of the best black actors in Hollywood, including Harry Belafonte, whom he cast in his directorial debut. The two worked well together on *Buck and the Preacher* (1972), but Poitier still remained something of an object of scorn for those dissatisfied with the progress of the Civil Rights movement. One critic called the movie "a loose, amiable, post-Civil War Western with a firm though not especially severe Black Conscience. The film is aware of contemporary black issues but its soul is on the plains once ridden by Tom Mix, whom Poitier, astride his galloping horse, his jaw set, somehow resembles in the majestic traveling shots given him by the director."

In spite of the criticism often thrown at him, Poitier used his stature in Hollywood to further the careers of a number of up-and-coming minority actors, including a young Bill Cosby, whom he cast in *Uptown Saturday Night* (1974). According to one critic, "Sidney Poitier [is] a man whose way with comedy is reminiscent of Stanley Kramer's in 'It's a Mad, Mad, Mad, Mad World.' It's less instinctive than acquisitive. He himself can't make anyone laugh but he knows people who can. Mr. Poitier has had the good sense to hire a lot of exceptionally talented and funny people, including Richard Wesley, who wrote the screenplay for 'Uptown Saturday Night.' Mr. Poitier's intelligence and taste are most noticeable in the film's casting, in the leeway he gives his actors, and in his ability at times to make himself seem physically small and downright intimidated. For a man of his stature, that cannot be easy." Poitier also directed and starred with Cosby in *Let's Do it Again* (1975), a film that earned him the Image award for Best Director from the National Association for the Advancement of Colored People.

Bill Cosby

During this time in his life, Poitier began dating Joanna Shimkus, a Canadian actress, and the two married in 1976 and went on to have two children together: Anika and Sydney Tamiia. They remain married to this day.

Poitier next worked with Cosby on *A Piece of the Action* (1977), a film that finally earned him the respect he deserved as a director. Critics praised the movie, with one saying, "Sidney Poitier has done it again…But he has done it with a difference, an obvious social purpose and a new name: 'A Piece of the Action.' In short, Mr. Poitier has provided something for just about everyone, including those who might be concerned about the question of all this moralizing coming from a character who is introduced as a criminal. 'A Piece of the Action' is firmly on the side of the angels. It is possible to criticize its lack of originality and its transparent slickness; but these are flaws that must be balanced against its evident craftsmanship, its entertainment and its social conscience."

By the time Poitier was directing *Stir Crazy* (1980), Cosby was in such demand that he was unavailable to appear in the movie, and that turned out to be lucky for the younger actor because critics panned the movie. One remarked, "'Stir Crazy' ... is a prison comedy of quite stunning humorlessness, considering its cast and that it was directed by Sidney Poitier, who has a couple of raffishly attractive comedies to his credit...What appears on the screen, though, appears to have been improvised, badly, more often than written." To Poitier's credit, even if critics didn't care for the film, audiences loved it, and it proved to be one of the highest moneymaking films of all time.

On the other hand, *Hanky Panky* (1982) bombed at the box office and elicited the following reaction from one disgruntled critic: "Sidney Poitier's 'Hanky Panky'...is an out-of-breath suspense-comedy that is apt to leave you far less exhilarated than exhausted, but that comment is made with a certain amount of hesitancy...'Hanky Panky'...is virtually one long chase sequence that begins in Manhattan, goes to Boston, makes a short detour to Maine and winds up in the Arizona desert after a wild flight over the Grand Canyon."

In addition to directing and starring in his own movies, Poitier starred in few more films during the 1980s and 1990s. Among these was *Sneakers* (1992), which earned him a nomination for the Image Award for Outstanding Actor in a Motion Picture. He also starred in the sequel *To Sir, with Love II* (1996), as well as *The Jackal* (1997), with the latter earning him a Blockbuster Entertainment Award for Favorite Supporting Actor.

As the end of the millennium approached, Poitier became reflective about his work in Hollywood, saying, "I've been a principal player in motion pictures for more than 50 years. That's a longevity that makes a statement. And my body of work in those 50 years is a testament to those producers who had the courage to step out during the tough years. It's a testament to my values...I am never too rushed to give someone an autograph...I will stop. And if I'm running to catch a plane, I will say to the person, 'Please jog with me.' I don't want to be the agent of passing that feeling [of rejection] to anybody."

Chapter 9: His Best Self

"We all have different selves: There is a public self, a private self and a core self. We all know the public self—it's how we put our best foot forward, smiling and behaving. But the private self is a more fundamental self, and that is where we find our frailties, our fears. It's like a clearinghouse where our demons are safe. Then there's the core self, which is our pure instinct. That's where all our goodness and capacity for kindness lives. You can feel it sometimes. When people say, "I feel it in my stomach," that's the core self. Our best comes from there, and we know how courageous and honorable we are. The core self is who we are." – Sidney Poitier

"So it's been kind of a long road, but it was a good journey altogether." - Sidney Poitier

In 1999, Poitier was asked what he would like to do with the remainder of his life, and he thoughtfully responded, "I'd like to write, act, teach, lecture—anything creative. I must also service my curiosity. I want to continue to wonder about things, because there is a young man inside me, and he is energetic and mentally active. I can examine so many things. I would like to do independent thinking about everything—to just sit and think independently about things." Fortunately, his years of excellent work opened many doors for him to do just that.

During the 1990s, Poitier began to make rare appearances on television shows, careful to only choose projects that he believed were worth his time and effort. One of his first appearances was as Thurgood Marshall in the docudrama *Separate but Equal* (1991), a performance that earned him nominations for a Primetime Emmy Award for Outstanding Lead Actor in a Miniseries or a Movie and a Golden Globe Award for Best Actor in a Miniseries or Television Film. Likewise, his portrayal of Gypsy Smith in *Children of the Dust* (1995) garnered him a nomination for an Image Award for Outstanding Actor in a Television Movie, Mini-Series or Dramatic Special. His role as the South African leader Nelson Mandela in *Mandela and de Klerk* (1997) garnered him the most praise, with five award nominations, and his title role in *The Simple Life of Noah Dearborn* won him another Image Award, this time for Outstanding Actor in a Television Movie, Mini-Series or Dramatic Special.

In addition to his television appearances, Poitier has continued to write well into his 80s. In 1980, his published his first autobiography, called simply *This Life*. He followed it in 2000 with *The Measure of a Man: A Spiritual Autobiography* and in 2008 with *Life beyond Measure – letters to my Great-Granddaughter*. The latter became an Oprah's Book Club selection, and he eloquently wrote what he hoped the book would teach his great-granddaughter: "I want my great-granddaughter to have a fairly good understanding of the world in which I lived for 81 years and also the world before I came into it - all the way back a hundred thousand years, to the beginning of our species." Poitier even completed his first novel, *Montaro Caine*, in 2013.

One thing Poitier does not enjoy is being asked questions about issues related to race. He once publicly stated, "I deal with race-based questions all the time, but I resent them. I will not let the press thrust me into a definition by feeding me only race questions. I've established that my concern with race is substantive. But at the same time, I am not all about race. I have had to [deal with this] all my career. And I've had to find balance. So much was riding on me as one of the first blacks out there. It's been an enormous responsibility. And I accepted it, and I lived in a way that showed how I respected that responsibility. I had to. In order for others to come behind me, there were certain things I had to do." Understandably, Poitier seems to feel that he did his part to advance opportunities for minorities during his acting career: "Every one of those pictures, with the exception of ... two ... came from filmmakers who had to make a comment that racism is wrong. There are people—black, white, blue, green—who find it necessary to make that kind of comment through their lives or professions. And I was a part of that mix. I was privy to the big picture—a lot of people aren't."

Of course, much of Poitier's time continues to be taken up with his duties as the Bahamian ambassador to Japan, a position he had held since 1997. He is also his country's ambassador to the United Nations Educational, Scientific and Cultural Organization.

As is typically the case with aging actors, Poitier's recent years have seen him receive a number of honors and lifetime achievement awards. In 2001, he was given an Honorary Academy Award for his contribution to American cinema, and he was also recently presented with the Lincoln Medal. He later recalled, "I was overjoyed, for obvious reasons. It was an evening that I never thought would come in my lifetime. I'm glad it did, because I could use that as a peg around which I can articulate my appreciation of my country."

Ernest Borgnine's death in 2012 has left Poitier as the oldest living man to have won an Academy Award for Best Actor, and that title carries certain privileges, including the opportunity in 2014 to appear on stage with Angelina Jolie to present the Best Director Oscar at the 86th Academy Awards ceremony. Following a standing ovation in his honor, Poitier made a short speech encouraging his fellow actors to "keep up the wonderful work."

Now 87, Poitier is often asked about his thoughts on the twilight of his life. On occasion, he has been humorous about it, once joking, "Far as I can tell, I still have most of my hair, my gut is not hanging over my belt, and I still have all of my teeth." But not surprisingly, he also remains hopeful: "I would like to die like my mother did. She was walking about the house, and she said to my sister, 'Make me a cup of tea and bring it to me, I'm going to take a nap.' It took my sister two or three minutes to get the tea, and when she walked into the bedroom, my mother was gone. She was gone in three minutes, and that was a blessing. I hope I'm that deserving…I'd like to meet my end with grace. I shall certainly try my best to meet it with grace. There is always the element of anxiety about it, but that anxiety lessens over the years…If you are anxious about death, then you don't have a sense of the oneness of things—you feel that after death, you will be no more."

It's a safe bet to assume Poitier will always maintain his sense of grace.

Poitier after receiving the Presidential Medal of Freedom in 2009

Bibliography

Goudsouzian, Aram. Sidney Poitier: Man, Actor, Icon (2004).

Poitier, Sidney. This Life. Alfred a Knopf. (1980).

The Measure of a Man: A Spiritual Autobiography. Harper San Francisco. (2000).

Life Beyond Measure – letters to my Great-Granddaughter. Harper Collins. (2008).

Montaro Caine. Spiegel & Grau. (2013).